Reminders
from life, for life

Also by Roger Brown:

The Truth Seeker's Handbook
Themes of my Life
Reminders From Life for Life
Heading Out
Encounters
Insights
33 Years of Dreams

REMINDERS
from life, for life

from the
Truthseeker's Handbook

A collection of short journal entries that are perhaps philosophy if they are deep enough to qualify as that; references for daily living.

Roger Golden Brown

Golden Galaxy Publications

I can be contacted at the following e-mail address:
wordsmith@goldengalaxies.net

Visit my personal website:
https://goldengalaxies.net/

And check out my world affairs oriented website:
https://goldengalaxies.net/Quasar/

This book is available for sale at:
http://books2read.com/remindersfromlifeforlife

See all of my books at my Author Page:
http://books2read.com/rogergoldenbrown

Only the road and the dawn, the sun, the wind, and the rain,
And the watch fire under stars, and sleep, and the road again.

- John Masefield

Introduction

I was born to a British mother and a father whose family tree goes back to the 1500's in America. I grew up in the woods, north of Seattle. I was raised a Quaker. My father was an inspiration in every sense, a spiritually oriented man of high integrity. Also my entrance onto the Earth scene was timed to be someone born to be at the heart of the hippie movement and to contribute to helping the world change for the better. I was also born an Aquarian. And I embrace that as I identify physically as a world citizen and spiritually as a player in the greater scheme of things.

I have lived in many places, done quite a potpourri of work, and have known many unique individuals. Amidst the variety that spiced my life an integral part of a significant period of time was writing in journals. This started on San Jaun Island in Washington State in 1975. Through good times and hard times I wrote almost daily for over 20 years, recording observations, thoughts, feelings, dreams (both the nighttime and the aspirational varieties), and experiences; both physical experiences and some more etheric experiences.

Life is a trip. Amidst the uncertainties, during this journey, I have tried to at least be aware of what is going on around me and what is going on within me. Using entries from my journals and elaborating on them, I have put together writings that make up this and other books.

So… fellow sojourner. Welcome.

Reminders is in three parts:

- Reminders

- Shorty Reminders

- One Liner Reminders

Contents

Preface

When I reread my journals in order to log them and make them accessible I organized a group of entries that were meant as reminders to myself. From time to time I look at these and find myself reminded of things that I had seen so clearly at one particular moment, in one environment, and among certain circumstances in the flow of my life, and am often surprised; yeah, I knew that then.

Some of these reminders, whether regarding actions or attitudes, arose from contemplation and some from times I caught myself engaging in or featuring them and noticed the therapeutic benefit. I say therapeutic, but it is so much more than that. Many of these reminders are attitudes which clean house and give more space for the new and for necessary change.

It is so easy to forget and be swept along. Sometimes by events. Sometimes by the attitudes and agendas of other people we come into contact with. Sometimes by people we never meet but who seem to influence our society and make demands on our lives. But perhaps, mostly, by the pressures we put on ourselves relative to all the external things of one's life.

It will be noted by the shrewd reader that some of these reminders may seem to contradict each other. No doubt there is some truth to that. But each serves, I believe, to stimulate awareness of various aspects of life and various times and places along our paths. I leave them to be considered and applied when they seem helpful.

Many of these reminders mean something to me in the context of my life by just reading the one line title, but in putting this collection together I have expanded on each one a little. In the process of assembling these reminders, I find myself affected; finding myself more reflective. They seem to be having the effect that was the whole point of organizing this group of journal entries in the first place.

My hope is that they can be of some value to others as well.

Reminders

Decide to be Positive

Deciding to be positive is no small thing. I made a decision at one point in my life to turn over a new leaf; to decide to be positive. At that time many subtle things combined to make me feel like changing myself. I decided to profoundly change my vibration and thoroughly change my attitude and my daily behavior and responses to the events of the day. Much of it was of a spiritual nature; the awareness of something grander than the struggles of what non-dreamers like to refer to as "reality." So I just decided to glow; to vibrate at a higher vibration. I touched more. And I smiled a lot.

Almost immediately people seemed to respond to me differently. Without going into details, suffice to say that the world opened up to me in the weeks following that decision.

Now this arose organically from my life at that time but that does not mean that its lesson is any less valid or that it is not possible to manifest such a change by willing it at any time. There is always some "reality" that will pose a challenge if we decide to vibrate at a higher level, but we have the power of choice. Believing fully in this positive outlook and behavior is helpful, but short of that, to just act it and keep pushing yourself to outwardly express it can also yield results. Make yourself over in spirit.

Know that you are making it happen for yourself. Be forward and bold beautifully. When engaging with others, any words will do if you glow enough… and smile.

Pay Attention to Messages From the Universe

Think about dreams. Dreams are a symbolic play. Each character, each prop, and each act tell you something about yourself. They are symbolic, I believe, so that you have to participate in the sleuthing to unravel the mysteries of your own life. And as such they are an offered opportunity.

If you think about it life is full of such opportunities; messages that come in many forms and give us signs and information. When I first had the epiphany that made me aware of this as such a powerful tool I couldn't help but feel like I'd been a fool for not taking advantage of them. And that expression is really the key: take advantage of them.

But short of taking advantage of them, the first step is just to even recognize them and stop and say – woah, there is an opportunity. Even if you choose not to act on it, know it was offered and was there; something was offered to you and could be a tool to help you gain insight.

I made a list of where such messages might come from. By no means is this a complete list (I doubt there is such an animal) but a good starter.

- Dreams

- Bio-feedback – the body's response to things (everything and always, really)

- Emotional feedback – emotional response to things (everything and always)

- Chance meetings – encountering people

- Chance happenings – events or situations encountered

- Chance shared information – from any source - in person, TV, radio, book, computer

- Chance overhearings - something overheard in passing on the street or somebody talking in a restaurant or cafe, for example

Stay alert to messages from all quarters and make your own list.

Recognize the Issues and Dramas of Your Life as Part of Your Own Particular Style

If you can accept the nature of progressing through life's days as your own style, it can help to bring the responsibility for your actions home. Responsibility sounds heavy and maybe burdensome, but with accepting that it is your own style comes also the opportunity to apply your own unique approach to the possibilities of dealing with whatever you need to. It's your game. Try and make the rules work for you. And maybe, above all, don't let others define your approach to dealing with things. It is, after all, your life.

Advice from others is ok. Listening is good. But don't accept others' advice and solutions straight out. Try them on, see how they fit. And tailor them to your style.

It's your life. Validate and empower your style, your approach, your solutions.

 Roger Golden Brown

Seek to be in the Center of Your Life

Be in the here and now. You've heard it said a thousand times. But more than that, be in the center of your life. Be inside your life. More than just taking part in life, you are the place it all comes from. The source.

Imagine the despair of someone not consciously participating in life. Just being done to. Instead, validate your life and the creativity of your choices. It's you. Live life like the game is afoot. In high school I ran cross country and before the race began I'd be all nervous and out-of-sorts. I'd feel tight and awkward until the starting gun went off, then I was suddenly free - I was doing it. It was up to me. Working things out thrills me; wondering what will happen irks me and drags me.

Be on a mission.

Be in the center of your life; in time and in space. Be hungry but be careful that your longing for something doesn't lead you away from the center of your life to somewhere or something you hope or expect to be.

Don't wait for the "whens" and the "if onlys", thinking or believing that once something happens, then you'll whatever. Contribute to life somehow; your life, all life. If life isn't flowing, develop a course of action, do the best you can, trust nature, carry on. If you need time out to emote, grieve, or feel it to give up, allow yourself that; but temporarily.

Soak Up the Good That Comes Your Way and Let the Unpleasant Slip By

There was a time when I was very aware of myself struggling with unpleasant feelings. And I remembered an old philosophy of mine. And that was that as I passed through time and space, to absorb and go with the good coming my way and to let the bad slide by. I would feature an image of myself standing straight and broad when I encountered something good and desirable so as to take it in and absorb it and feel it fully and when I encountered something unpleasant I would turn a side to it and make myself narrow, making it easier for it to slip by.

Singing Out Loud is of Tremendous Benefit to the Soul

This is not earth shaking news, but, I believe, a simple truth. Singing out loud is of tremendous benefit to the soul. Do it often. It works on so many levels. It can be a distraction from worry. Or perhaps it's a better use of words to think of it as a replacement for worry. I don't think it's healthy to deny and suppress issues but incessant worry eats away at body and soul, and singing out loud can take you to a different place. Also there is the actual resonance. There is healing in sound and vibration.

Choose Times of Music and Sound Receptivity; Not Louding Upon the World

Another reminder suggested singing out loud. So now I suggest not singing out loud. Go figure. There is a time and place for everything. I had an experience once when I was singing along with some music when I had a touch of laryngitis and it was uncomfortable so I decided to just listen. I became aware that the music became more crystalline as I changed my energy to receptiveness. And, continuing on through the day as I consciously chose to be quiet and still my larynx, I became aware of acoustics and much of the subtle nature of my surroundings. To be quiet consciously is not just quiet non-speaking moments, but an attitude of not projecting, not louding upon the world. An attitude of receptiveness.

And applied in another way, I was with a friend of mine who is a real talker (enjoyably so) and instead of responding and pitching in and head tripping on and on with him, I just nodded my head and took it in. My awareness of him and his message; his style; the unique life that he has came clearer to me. Occasional larynx-free days or periods of time can really enhance appreciation.

     Roger Golden Brown

Say Hello to People as Spirits

I must admit that I don't say hello to people as spirits enough. I do, in some moods, in some spaces, but all too often I'm engulfed in the physical; reacting to their acting. Or perhaps trying to understand their psychology behind their behavior.

These ways of thinking about and viewing others is often a reaction to wanting to understand why things aren't as we feel they should be; whether it's somebody we are close to or a stranger on the street or even a part of our society that is disturbing to us. This has the effect of making us in some way demanding.

See people as spirits. Free them to their potential. That sounds quite altruistic, as there are certainly many individuals whose actions seem destructive or obtrusive. But, truth is, it only clutters their space and muddles their ability to grow when we reduce someone to being nothing more than their acts and their personality. Disagreement is fine. It's part of living socially. But remain aware of the role they play as spirits on the same stage we all share.

This sounds like it is all about making nice for the sake of others, but seeing others as spirits helps remind us that we ourselves are spirits and helps us stay on the high road.

Love Everyone Always Because… Who Knows?

Loving everyone in an altruistic way is certainly a good practice. But in terms of everyday encounters with other humans we meet, there are some nuts and bolts things that need to be considered. Certainly we have and need to make choices regarding what vibrations we exist among and with whom we intimately co-mingle. And it is natural to want to be selective and check people out for fit first, before you invest much energy.

There have been times when I was so tired of loss and disappointment that I wanted to completely withdraw from the game. I retreated, believing that whoever is right for me I'll be certain about from the start. And I didn't want to deal with the complexities of the getting to know each other's trepidations. Or I was afraid of the disappointment.

But this really does take you out of the game. Not only do you have blinders on, but the walls are perceived by others. We really do need to take chances on hidden loving behind not so obvious faces if we expect that in return from the universe.

So, the bottom line is this. Appreciate people for what they have to offer; not just how they are now to you. You don't have to jump into relating to anyone but see them at face value, allow them to be, allow yourself to see them as dynamic and vital with qualities and capabilities and not just how they fit you right at that moment.

So much for nuts and bolts. Complete the circle. Back to loving everyone always because…. who knows? It really is the high road. It is such a simple truth. Feel the love within. Don't think in terms of wanting anyone to be different or trying to change someone's mind. Instead, behave in such a way that you reach their hearts instead.

That should be enough for its own sake.

Also, maybe you are off your game and not seeing deeply enough. Maybe someone will surprise you and turn out to be someone you will value having in your life. Who knows?

Stay in Time, Allow Time's Natural Continuity

There was a week when I wanted time to go by fast; I was looking forward to something and was being impatient. And then when that week of waiting and being distracted by my impatience was over I wished I had gotten more done. There were a few things that really needed doing that I hadn't gotten done. What a fool I had been, thinking I could mess with time. It's always going to win.

Try to feel or maybe realize a sense of continuity in the events of your life. Be aware of the thread in the attitudes you hold regarding those events. Paradoxically, try to not try. Just allow it. Also paradoxically, taking time, not rushing, is the best way to get the most out of the precious time each of us has. Rhythm.

     Roger Golden Brown

Be a Human Being, Not a Human Doing

Doing is a fine thing. It is essential to life. But is life defined by our doing? I don't think so. That's too much of a burden to carry; to define ourselves by our doing. Don't get in the way of your essential purity. Don't push yourself into a model or characterize yourself by your doing.

Put another way, it's important to keep separate, in mind and attitude, life itself from the stuff of life. I once wrote in my journal, "I feel too stuck in my life to be me. 'My life' has become bigger than me." I had been looking at footage of Gene Kelly dancing and of a woman rock climbing and was feeling hurt and feeling self pity for all that I haven't done and never will do. This is, of course, a very human mood. But it is me judging myself by my doing. Not the being of my heart and soul.

Treat your life as an independent force.

Don't be Attached to Previous Successes (or Failures)

It's natural to want to repeat previous successes. It feels good to accomplish something of value and who can blame you for wanting to repeat that success. But life just doesn't work that way. The environment will always have changed in some way. Certainly, it's fine to apply the same skills or gifts in other ventures. But the energy and the act of the past is gone.

Once when I was replaying some event from my past and trying to get off on it, I felt how it wasn't clean; wasn't right. It came to me that past events are helpful when brought up to teach, show, give perspective to other events and to learn from about the linkages in one's own life. But to revel in them or try and relive them is a waste of time and energy. I came back to the present and felt more whole.

It's a subtle thing but there needs to be a certain level of non-attachment to free you to the same power you had in creating a successful experience in the first place. Feeling free of history and believing in what is flowing to and by and all around you gives you the clean slate to work on.

Using sports as an analogy, if you gloat and focus on the one great play you've just made, you'll miss the next opportunity. You've got to get back in the present and be enthused with what's facing you now. Playing music literally and in life metaphorically, you've got to let one note go to hear the next.

Likewise, feeling or believing that past failures or the time that has passed since peak moments indicates your life, is not true - quite the contrary; more likely they bind you to the old and used up. Interesting concept - we try and repeat the old successes and fret and struggle against past failures or

     Roger Golden Brown

losses, but hey!, they're used now. They're history. And who wants a used experience?

Live in Your Body, Not in Your Head

Be aware when engaging the mind. The mind is a great tool, but you should proceed with caution when it makes your decisions or dominates your behavior; particularly when communicating with others. Featuring logic or psychological thinking can severely hamper communications skills. The natural flow and timing can easily be overridden.

The head is meant to be visited. Unlike the body, there is no indoor plumbing to eliminate waste. When the mind is only visited it remains uncluttered so that fresh, creative, innovative thinking can be put to use. Sensory input is allowed to come in unmolested and will pass through beautifully. Old baggage, repeated thoughts, and old tape loops create dross and clog things up. And will eventually seep into the body.

It is true that the reflective mind has its role, but intellect, logic, philosophy, belief, and even values are easily corrupted, hypnotized, co-opted and perverted. The qualities of truth and goodness and health and righteousness are things you feel in your heart, in your gut. And in your muscles.

Live in your body; where truth is truth.

Recognize That Your Body is its Own Animal, You are its Steward

One night, lying in bed I had a powerful, clear, unique personal experience. I thought about my body and suddenly got this deep rush of compassion for my body and realized in that moment and glow that it's just ego to think that it's my slave; "my" body to do with as I choose. It is its own animal. As we are stewards of the earth, so are we stewards of our bodies. I felt shocked how I've assumed my dominion over it. I felt that I owed it many apologies. And I begged its understanding for my bumbling.

A corollary to this would be to realize that the body's natural state is to exist in radiant health. And that most of the pain and shortcomings and dis-eases of the body come from our mismanagement of it. Whether it be from foisting upon it, internally or externally, that which it has no use for and that which is toxic to it or whether it be from the stress we subject it to by our attitudes and anxieties.

Seek a harmonious relationship, recognizing the body's sovereignty and intelligence.

Don't Hide From or Suppress the Undesirable, Allow the Uncalculating Primitive

Once, when feeling completely incapable of effecting change in myself or in creating conditions in my life that would help bring change about, I wrote the following:

"I pollute my body with 'food' and constipate my system with a mental life that is addicted to the attachment to a personality that runs from shadow to shadow, forever eluding the golden light of my real self."

Be bold and aggressive and unafraid. You need not protect yourself from rejection or hurt or especially the loss of whichever face it is you feel you need to retain. You are a piece of art in the making. Believe that in any arena you can find a way. In a way it's a call to the primitive in us. Allow the uncalculating primitive. Do what needs to be done without being so calculating. To be sure, be careful to temper this freedom we all have with the creed of non-violence but flee the shadows and deal with whatever the light exposes. It is really the only way to tap the awesome personal power that is your birthright.

Do What Gives You Power in the Bigger Picture

If you look around and observe what people do, both unassuming acts and acts that are done as a statement of some sort, you may wonder why they choose to express themselves in such a manner. They are doing it because on some level they think it is effective.

We do things because we think it gives us power. Essentially that's what we all do, to some extent all the time; everything we do, every act. We do what we think gives us our power, brings us our power, leads us to our power.

Why then do we seem to waste our power or choose paths of denial and avoidance of positive responsible behavior.

That's the trap. We might waste time or act out physically in ways that fall short of our ideals or seem to exhibit a lack of introspection, but that is us choosing the short-sightedness of the avoidance of the pain or the discomfort of acts that challenge our status quo. Avoiding a challenge and the struggle to overcome the way we are can seem to give us more power than the outcome of the struggle would ultimately give us.

And perhaps the challenge in all growth and spiritual unfoldment is to recognize that the result of taking on challenges and breaking through will lead to a kind of harmony and flow and trust and faith that really does increase our power. Try and see the bigger picture.

Stay Aware of What Your Own Energy Is

Do your best to be in your body and to be free of others' energy.

First, learn to be fully present in your own body and endeavor to stay in your own body. Take stock of yourself from head to toe. Try to not be "spaced out" or distracted. Tip the balance of what occupies your mind towards an awareness of your senses and your physical surroundings rather than the thoughts in your head.

Endeavor to know yourself. Just think, if you really knew yourself; really knew what is you and your creations for your life and your body, how effective you could be, both for yourself and others. The viewpoint would be so clear. It's like when hiking through the wild, how sometimes you need to find a high place to reconnoiter to help you decide what you best do or in what direction you best go.

Secondly, try and be aware of what is your own energy and what you may be picking up from those around you and the people closest to you in your life. The more you are in touch with your own body and in the present, the easier it is to recognize the energy that isn't your own.

It is completely natural to take on the energy of other people with whom we are in contact. This is part of communicating. But if you are not aware of or lose awareness of what energy is yours and what is theirs, it can be disconcerting and unhealthy. It is confusing to feel someone else's pains, physical or emotional; their created reality.

Think about how we all have our own unique chosen realities; our bodies, pains, parents, astrology and histories. Just imagine what a shock it would be to trade bodies with someone else. To suddenly deal with someone else's stuff would be pretty demanding and probably not very

 Roger Golden Brown

comfortable. If you take on someone else's energy, you don't have the context to deal with it.

I feel like I should mention here that being consolidated in your own body does not, in fact, isolate you in the sense that you are not or cannot be one with others in a spiritual sense or human sense. In fact it is actually a paradox that the better you know your self, the more easily and effectively you can participate with all. And when you are not taking on the drama that someone else is involved in, you are in a better position to help that person, should you choose to.

Release Others to Their Greater Good

Releasing others to their greater good is a powerful tool.

To hold someone in contempt is a selfish act. And destructive for all parties involved. By doing so the other person is constantly carrying your bad vibes and you are contributing to any difficulty they may have achieving and moving towards their greatest good. Make a bit of a ritual about it. Don't just think it; really release them to their own unfettered unfoldment.

If you feel anger or disappointment towards anyone, first love yourself for feeling that way and look for the truth that by loving yourself and not feeling bad about it, you free yourself to your goodness. Then release them. It may not solve all the issues, but it lightens the load for everyone.

Focus on the Strengthening of Yourself and Your Own Ideals

The need for recognition seems to be a fundamental human quality. I believe, however, that ultimately, as an individual, as a participant in this great experiment on this planet, it is important to seek a place within where you have very little need for recognition.

What's important is to validate yourself for simply being who you are and what you give and not to care about what you get back. The thing is to participate and share what you do and how you feel without feeling that your center (your self) is compromised. And don't judge what you're giving by what others are receiving or what you are by what others are perceiving. Ultimately you have no control over that.

Also when confronted with the ugly or undesirable, try and not fight against it. Rather, focus on the strengthening of yourself and your own ideals. We function better in life when we are flexible. Flexibility is easier when it's not indicative of, or seen as, a compromise of self; easier when you're not changing because you think you ought to or you need to, in order to fit something or someone else's ideas or ideals.

Seek the Sources of Problems but Recognize That Things Springing From the Source Can Take on a Life of Their Own

In an interview I once heard somebody say: Drugs are not the source of the problem, but they take on a life of their own. This concept could be applied to many habits, relationship patterns, arguments, and socially indoctrinated living styles. Even the machines and mechanics of our lifestyle choices.

Like if you are depressed about something so you feel like just sitting around instead of taking your daily walk. The indolence and the lack of exercise are consequences of the way you deal with the depression, but they take on a life of their own. Inertia has a way of growing and the longer you go without exercise, the less you feel like doing it.

So if you catch yourself in any kind of destructive behavior, seek the cause or root of it; ultimately identifying the source is important. But, having taken on a life of its own, working on overcoming bad habits or responses to the original issue also has merit. It keeps the situation from being compounded and it helps remove obstacles to identifying and dealing with the source issue.

One very practical example is stress. Stress itself is unhealthy in many ways. And it's easy to say you are stressed because you have so much to do or because of this or that. But think – is that really the source of the stress? Often the answer is no; that itself isn't inherently stress producing. The event that seem to be the cause of the stress isn't usually the source of the stress, but the stress has taken on a life of its own. Work on mollifying the stress in order to circle back and find its roots.

     Roger Golden Brown

Never Hate Yourself

After having been in a phase of feeling really in tune, I noticed how as my rhythm failed I got down on myself. I began saying negative things about myself. It really struck me deeply as I became aware of it.

It really struck me that you should just never put yourself self down. But how do you deal with being disappointed in yourself or observing yourself making choices that you are critical of?

I would say try try try to love anything you can. Yourself if you can. If you can't, someone else maybe. If you can't, the weather maybe. Or how you were. A choice you once made. A time you helped someone. Or even a time you accepted help. Anything.

You have a right to be here and there are no requirements. Your existence alone is valuable. Just don't hate yourself. The consequences and implications are so extensive.

So, let me say this:

Never, ever, under any circumstance, for any reason, no matter what, under any conditions, ever, regardless, absolutely, ever, at anytime, anywhere, with or because of anybody or any event, ever dislike yourself.   Got it??!!!

Avoid Adding Fire to Issues Being Discussed, Allow Others to Save Face

Suppressing issues out of fear of the conflict is unhealthy and makes most situations just get worse. Bring things up without being in conflict mode. Don't assume an issue will be a conflict. As a participant, we have a lot of power to defuse potentially hot issues.

It's often the case that the problem is more in the consequences of avoiding bringing things up than in the original issue. Many apparent disagreements are not irreconcilable and turn out to be just social blunders and not really problems as such. Look for opportunities to laugh together at the misunderstandings. Sometimes two people just have different ideas about the implications of a certain act and when it's understood what it means to each of them, it's not that hard to find a middle ground.

Avoid adding fire to conversations by not correcting people if they measure you incorrectly. Avoid giving your opinion when it adds fire to a critical conversation just because you feel a need to defend yourself or your position. Feeling like you have to defend yourself only creates an us vs. them tenor to the discussion.

And one of the most powerful tools in conflict resolution is to allow others to save face. Sometimes, especially when some issue has grown over time, people will really begin to own a certain stance. Seeking a way to resolve the issue while not openly calling the other person out for their stance helps a lot to soften the middle ground.

Quietly, within yourself, forgive the other person (and yourself) without insisting on an apology, regardless of your actual appraisal of the sources of the issue. Realize that you possess a power that no one else can take away from you.

If You Feel the Need to be in Control, Try Instead to be in Awareness

When feeling like life is running you around, it is easy to have a sense of futility or despair. You feel out of control, vulnerable to influences that are taking you places you don't really want to go. This is bound to happen at times. Most likely it has to do with lack of flexibility. I don't mean the that your lack of flexibility is causing the events or forces that are taking you for a ride, but rather your flexibility determines how bumpy the ride is.

There are ways and techniques that a person can employ to have more control; visualization, imagination, trying to orchestrate or perhaps choreograph the events. (Or, of course, you could try and push back against the forces with your own force – good luck on that one.)

But the fact of the matter is, you really can't control in totality all of what is going on around and with you. Although we all possess a certain amount of power and we all play our own parts in directing events, there are just too many other people and other external forces at play.

So, when you feel the need to be in control, try instead to be in awareness. In awareness you can best function utilizing yourself during any experience. Although you have free will, so do others around you so there are no guarantees. But… the more aware you are of the physical forces at play and the vibrations and intentions of the people at play, the better equipped you are to find a comfortable groove.

And the more your awareness increases, the higher your vibration will be, which allows you to kind of buzz around within the chaos of the world and find the spaces amidst its juggernaut.

The Oversight Principle

In a conversation with a friend of mine he said he wanted to stop stumbling along, just trying to make spiritual sense out of events as they occurred. He wanted to stop just acting out of habit and was inspired by some Rudolph Steiner he had been reading to apply himself more scientifically towards spiritual goals; to make conscious choices.

That reminded me of two lessons in my life.

The first was when I was with two others, one of who was looking all over for something they had lost; looking kind of haphazardly and undirected. The other man, named Don Overstreet was someone I knew to be pretty analytical; more so than appeals to me. But he said something to the man who was floundering in his search that has stuck with me. He said, Stop. Right where you are. Look around. Take stock of the situation. Think. Proceed rationally.

That so impressed me that I have, employing a word play, named it The Oversight Principle, oversight having two quite different meanings. It can mean to fail to see something. But it also means to watch over or tend something.

Far beyond just trying to find something, the Oversight Principle can be employed in many arenas of life. One such case would be when a physical ailment appears. Instead of simply ruing the discomfort or impairment, seek whence it came. Stop and ask yourself when it was that you first noticed it, are there other related symptoms or feelings, how were you feeling emotionally then and now. Or when you find yourself reacting to a situation, stop and take a moment to track the situation. What led to this situation, what actions or events brought you to this point. In the case of an issue with a person, take a breath and look at the thread in the events or perhaps in a conversation and try and get a clear idea of the

 Roger Golden Brown

bigger picture. Use the Oversight Principle also when reflecting on things in general. There is inevitably a series of events or thoughts or something that offers insight into where you now are.

The second lesson I was reminded of is the story of the person who is dedicated to progressing and achieving a goal with all good intentions and climbs strong and skillfully up a tree, but didn't take the time or have the presence of mind to realize he was going up the wrong tree.

Delight in Truth at all Costs

Everything that is experienced must be accepted. Simply say, yes, this is happening to me. We tend to avoid and repress and choose against less pleasant feelings. What a rip-off! These selfsame unpleasant feelings are important information as to what is going on; they hold the key to why we don't at the moment have pleasant feelings. They are, in fact, the feelings needing the most attention.

Delight in truth at all costs. It is always an opportunity. Validating the truth reveals the way out of the fog and into the light. Stated simply, if you don't know where you are, how can you get to where you'd like to go.

Having said that, it is not always easy to know what the truth is; especially when it has been hidden in denial for a long time. But we mustn't be afraid and must be truth seekers.

One way that the avoidance of truth expresses itself is in the body as pain or discomfort. When a part of your body is complaining or hurting don't just wish it away. And don't blame the messenger. Ask yourself what the message is. Validate what you are feeling and follow the clues.

"Seek and ye shall find." Yeah, right! Well it is right but not always, or even often, easy. But we must stay at it. It is also true that like everything else practice improves our ability. The oftener we seek, the easier and more natural that seeking becomes. Plus as we retrieve more of our truth from the shadows and from denial, the less muck there is to obscure it.

Don't Get Caught in the Looking for Results Trap

Although it is natural or at least normal for people to rate their existence and their time on earth in terms of results, it can be counterproductive to be looking for results and placing results as the highest priority.

It seems that in the ever accelerating rat race of these modern times that our and many societies have become, action and accomplishment is highlighted. And it seems our fellow rats are moving faster all the time seeking goals that are ever more remote. This cannot be good for the heart and soul, or for our bodies.

From a spiritual viewpoint perhaps having no goals of accomplishments is of more value. Live in and for the moment. Perhaps what's more important is having a good heart and a quiet mind. That, also, should align, strengthen, and heal the body. Seek peace.

I think there is a middle ground. I would agree that there is something to be said for being able to reflect on one's life and feel proud of what you have accomplished. Having goals is not in and of itself destructive; just don't get caught in the looking for results trap. It is all circular. It is ok to value accomplishments but a good heart and a peaceful mind should come first.

I would suggest that having a goal in sight but focusing on the means rather than the end actually makes the accomplishing of goals more likely. Also, part of the trap of looking for results is that if those results are too tightly defined, it may get in the way of having unexpected but equally valuable or more valuable results as the outcome.

Adopt a Child's View of Life

Watching some children one day something occurred to me; a natural condition of their lives that would naturally give them a life perspective that we as adults have lost. Or maybe I should say, quite literally have grown out of.

Children are quite obviously in a constant state of change. They are growing. Up. On the surface, they take it for granted. Paradoxically, they are very aware of their growth. I'm bigger than I was last year. Next year I'll be as big as older bro or sis is now. Hey, I can reach the lowest branch of that tree and climb it now; I couldn't do that last summer. This offers them the optimism and belief that many things may be achievable in the future that are not now possible. Also skills and talents develop and improve as their bodies' capabilities improve and also as they accumulate experience and exposure to more and more new things.

I think, as adults, we buy into a kind of static situation. We fret that we can't do certain things, thinking, I haven't been able to do that up till now; what reason do I have to believe that will change. We worry about conditions that need not be permanent. Our bodies seem less supple and less responsive to challenges and we accept that. Although there may be certain changes in the exuberance of the bodies we inhabit as adults, I think they are far less restricted than we have come to believe. And, I believe that our attitudes all too often support that belief and probably to a great extent are responsible for the creating of the conditions that make us feel more sluggish in body and spirit. Thus we create self fulfilling prophesies.

Adopt an attitude of openness. Don't buy in to cannot. Even as we may develop conditions that really can't change, as long as there is life there is a place to grow. Seek

     Roger Golden Brown

enthusiasm. Allow what is but assume change. Assume it as a natural quality of life. And give it the benefit of the doubt that the change can be for the better.

Check it Out: Does This Bring me Pleasure?

What is the meaning of life? What is important? Does this have value? The answer is in another question. Does this bring me pleasure? Does this feel good?

It will be argued that a philosophy of seeking pleasure is a recipe for a hedonistic no good lifestyle. The question is are you up to it? Have you matured yourself enough to recognize real pleasure? Not frivolous behavior that leaves you with a hangover, be it of the body or spirit. That which brings you real pleasure will always be something of value. Cheating and lying may offer you a temporary gain and one might find a corrupted pleasure in that, but the pitfalls and traps are many. That ain't true pleasure.

Things that bring true pleasure have no down sides. Not necessarily no complications or struggles as we unravel ourselves, but you will be enhancing your life and your progress.

How could doing what is right not work? How could doing what really feels good not be good for you. It makes no sense on any level that our hearts and bodies would be so constructed that pleasure would be something to be avoided. Pleasure is simply the smooth functioning of a being.

Try and create a life of things that feel good. Of course in a multifaceted world and society and personal life you can't always do things on your feel good list. Just do the best you can. Say prayers. Be reflective. Don't ever abandon love or loving. Trust in nature.

Become selfless. Give freely. Discover the pleasure of giving.

Become selfish. Hunger for the pleasure of giving.

Aesthetics and Values Will Carry You
When Knowing Can't

Watching college age kids in the park one day I was thinking how you can't expect them or children to really know themselves, to recognize the threads in society and in the world. Most of them simply haven't had enough twists and turns in the road or perhaps the demands of adulthood to have a feeling for how life unfolds. And you can't really expect them to have communication down, to have matured communication in a wide variety of circumstances with others.

Wisdom does come with age. Or actually I should say wisdom can come with age; the passing of years offers more and more opportunity to gain wisdom that can be used for the betterment of all.

But, as I was watching those kids in the park I saw something else. I saw clearly that each one of them has, regardless of age, an innate ability to be aware of aesthetics and values. And it was also clear to me that those really are enough. More than enough, they are necessary. They will carry you when knowing can't. What's more, aesthetics and values will be the vehicle that will transform experience into wisdom.

Shorty Reminders

- ✔ Get into it. Get past the cliché. Really get into it. Get inside. Slow time down and get in step with whatever you are doing, seeing, hearing, feeling, smelling, touching, or imagining.

- ✔ Daydream fantasies. Creative visualization. Trepidation. Fear. Whatever. You are what you think about all day.

- ✔ Ultimately you can't make someone do something against their will. I'm not sure if I really believe that, but assume that it is true or that you wouldn't want to because it is not right. If you can't make anyone love you, seek out your company, have sex with you, give you money, and so on, what you can do is change your own vibration so it seems desirable for others to find the option of you favorable.

- ✔ De-crystallize. If you state an opinion, learn something, or make a mistake, there's no reason to feel bad or proud. It's not you. It's just something you did, or said, but you don't own the past and it doesn't own you. It's one of those cool paradoxes though. You can't use that as an excuse to not be responsible. You've just gotta stay free and sensible.

✔ Don't be smug because of having things, material or otherwise, in your life. These satisfactions and creature comforts ought to be recognized as the means, not the end.

✔ Never believe that what you say is what you communicate. Be aware that what is heard by others when you speak to them isn't necessarily what you said; at least not in meaning or intent. Without being on the same wavelength or in some profound way having worked out a common lexicon based on experience, it's probably an illusion that they have any idea what you truly mean, where you are really coming from in your realm of experience when you put your well chosen favorite words together.

✔ Being in a positive space is obviously fertile ground for success. Experience has taught me, however, that there is something more effective. Seek instead to remove the negative, leaving you in a neutral space, where all things naturally take place.

✔ Mood and attitude is everything. To try and change the physical first is like the trailer trying to pull the tractor. Or perhaps like the trailer trying to push the tractor.

✔ Happiness and loneliness are not necessarily mutually exclusive. It's possible to be happy and

   Roger Golden Brown

still be lonely. A person in a general state of happiness can experience loneliness. Loneliness happens. It's part of the richness of being human.

✔ No matter how much you may doubt that you have a worthy talent or skill, it just ain't so. Look high, look low. Don't leave any stone unturned. Don't think anything is insignificant. Get to know your style. Do what you're good at. It looks good on you. It fits you well. It is an opportunity to shine without trying too hard.

✔ A place in your heart and soul isn't enough. There must be a place in your life or it isn't happening. Look to your heart and soul for that which you desire, then do what you need to find or make a place in your life for it.

✔ Change is inevitable. It is movement and that is the very stuff of life. And since it is inevitable why resist it. That's where the pain starts. If you feel the urge to fight change, take a moment, step back, and see where it is going to the best of your awareness. Realize that change is not only inevitable, but that change itself is good and natural. By first accepting it, this gives you the opportunity to participate in the change and help shape the outcome.

✔ Admit the limits of your awareness and senses, ask and pray for magic. Accept it without having to understand it or feel personally responsible for it.

One Liner Reminders

✔ God allows us mistakes to build character. I forget sometimes.

✔ When you do it right it's gone, when you do it wrong, it's still there.

✔ Happiness is the relation between what one imagines their needs to be and what one imagines to have.

✔ Reality is synonymous with power. Relax and expand.

✔ If you don't do it, it won't get done.

✔ You can't steal 2nd with one foot on 1st.

✔ Undirected will becomes frustration.

✔ Feel stuck? Feel restless? Go out and make some mistakes today.

✔ You can't go swimming by looking at the lake.

✔ Want to feel good, instead of wanting something to happen so you will feel good.

✔ Fear mustn't be the reason for strength in solitude.

✔ All ideas are valid.

✔ Life is hard enough without thinking it's hard. Keep moving.

✔ Time is yours to live within; on your own terms.

✔ Relearn, re-integrate in new applications, under new circumstances.

✔ Instead of thinking, "it's like this", think, "that's one element of a bigger picture."

✔ Pain is only felt in resistance.

✔ Never judge the limits of what you can do, until there's no turning back.

✔ Love the process, you can't own anything.

✔ How does it feel in your gut?

✔ Act with the certainty that you have when the chips are down because hey, the chips are always down.

✔ Don't let fear make your decisions for you.

✔ Giving is receiving.

     Roger Golden Brown

- ✔ Appreciate everyone's individual perception.

- ✔ Be true to the best you know, and the next will be given to you.

- ✔ It's ok to make a mistake doing something you feel you need to do.

- ✔ Repeat after me: I am, I can, and I don't have to.

- ✔ Forgive the past, keep clear the present, forgive the past.

- ✔ What you create for yourself, you create for the world. (and visa versa)

- ✔ Be unrealistic. Ask for what you want.

- ✔ Careful, now. Don't get so involved in the physical that you expect it to rescue you.

- ✔ Simplify and be happy. Fewer moving parts; less to go wrong.

- ✔ Be on a mission. Stay in school. Whether your school has walls or not.

- ✔ When a parade blocks your way, the only way to get past is to join in and pretend you're part of it for a while as you work your way to the other side.

✔ It's alright to be disappointed in someone. It's not alright to hold them responsible for your disappointment.

✔ If you don't know what you know because you know it, you don't really know it.

✔ A ship is safe as long as it stays in port, but that's not what ships are built for.

✔ Treat your life as an independent force.

✔ Not making connections is a sin of the mind.

✔ No matter how much pain you may be in, recognize the cosmos and commune.

✔ As soon as you are ready to accept something, you don't need to.

✔ Unused potential is a morbid thing.

✔ He who lives by the sword, dies by the sword. He who lives by the mind, dies by the mind. If you must use your brain, try and wonder about things rather than think about them.

✔ If you want to know your future, look at your present and see what survives.

✔ The unknown always conditions the known.

- ✔ Believe in yourself…. for Christ's sake.

- ✔ Genius corresponds with enthusiasm; it all opens up.

- ✔ The alignment you have when you express yourself determines the power your expression will have.

- ✔ When you have loosened the winds, you must abide by their blowing.

And finally...

- ✔ Be Excellent To Each Other

About the Author

I was born in Seattle and spent the first 30 years of my life in the Pacific Northwest. Well, except for 4 school years in a private Quaker boarding school in Pennsylvania, which was a great communal living experience. I think this had a far reaching and profound effect on my life. I have since lived in many different places, mostly favoring the West Coast; Olympia, Bellingham, San Juan Island, San Luis Obispo, Santa Cruz, Santa Fe, Maui, Kauai and currently Sebastopol, California. Integral in my experience has been a number of trips to Europe, mostly spending my time in the area around Innsbruck, Austria, which is my second home and where I have so many dear friends.

Work has also been varied; most of it being for myself. I have worked as a carpenter and with a partner built 2 houses in the mountains (one in Idaho, one in Washington) using (almost) exclusively hand tools. In Santa Cruz, I started my own business building and selling portable massage tables of my own design and did that for many years.

I love music; my favorites being classical music of the more sublime nature (Debussy, for one) and psychedelic era rock of which I consider the Beatles to be the ultimate. My favorite instrument is the human voice. Music has been a cornerstone of my life and has carried me through many peaceful and turbulent times.

I love to get out and ramble around on my mountain bike. It keeps me young; not the exercise so much as the playfulness and freedom of it.

And my most recent passion is playing strategic eurogame board games with friends..

Other Books by Roger Brown

The Truth Seeker's Handbook has been published in print and as an eBook. I kept journals for over 20 years, writing almost every day. Much of the philosophy, the struggles leading to learning and the attitudes that helped me get through life appears in this book. It has a section dealing with major life themes, one about our relationship to the Earth, one retelling stories of serendipity, and finally a section of reminders to help along the way.

Two of those sections are available as their own books:

Themes of my Life
Reminders From Life for Life

Excerpt from The Truth Seeker's Handbook:

Delight in truth at all costs. We really must accept everything we experience. Simply say, yes, this is happening to me. We tend to avoid and repress and choose against less pleasant feelings. What a rip-off! They offer powerful information as to what is going on; information as to the reason why we don't at the moment have pleasant feelings. The desirable feelings validate flow and rightness. The unpleasant ones are the ones needing the most attention.

- - -

Heading Out is poetry and prose and has been published in print and as an eBook. Cryptic and cosmic might be good words to describe these writings; word adventures. Poetry is an individual thing and I can't say for sure you will like them, but look for it and check out the free eBook sample.

A short poem from Heading Out:

Popsicle process brings freedom ... in heat.
What was ice yields a watery treat.
When we allow ourselves to have what we need
That water fertilizes and brings life to our seed.

- - -

Encounters has been published in print and as an eBook. It is about encounters with women in my life that were romantic and sometimes intimate but does not include the girlfriends or lovers of duration. It is all journal entries in real time; usually my initial feelings, the encounter evolving, and finally myself seeking resolution and completion for myself and hopefully us. These encounters took place mostly during my 20's and 30's and are very gutsy and emotional. I have been a very emotional person and it may surprise some people to read a man's feelings essentially unedited.

Excerpt from Encounters:

I approached her during a thunderstorm downpour on the main sunning deck (at Harbin Hot Springs). I was attracted to her and felt an immediate thrill from and affection for her. I wanted her. I spent some time with her and got to know her a little. I slept next to her on the sleeping deck. She let me know she needed space. She removed my hand gently from her body, but didn't let go. She held my hand a few moments more. What a beautiful softening of the space between us that she required. I was hurt and felt rejected, although I appreciated her communication and integrity. I cried. Strange sleep. Dreams. I felt again defeated but fought it, hung in there.

- - -

Insights has been published in print and as an eBook. This is a compilation of most of the journal entries which didn't appear in any of my other books, but that I felt needed to see the light of day. I organized them into such categories as Cosmic, Philosophy and Attitude, Love, Society, and several more.

Excerpt from Insights:

I heard Earth Angel on the radio today and thought about the American Dream and its surfacing in the 50's and the dreamy songs reflecting it. I was overwhelmed with a rush of rightness. Sure it is distorted. Sure its means are destructive. But the dream - to have comfort and ease and the time and space to relax and expand, time to create, to have comfortable homes is fine. It sparked a spiritual movement which unfortunately was complicated by an awesome opportunity to be corrupted by material and sensory numbing diversions. But the dream itself, it's not only the American Dream but a soul's dream. To mellow a life in a body. To find harmony. I'm all for it.

- - -

33 Years of Dreams has been published in print and as an eBook. Over a period of 33 years I wrote down a ton of dreams. A friend once said to me, why would anybody want to read anyone else's dreams? That got me to thinking but it came to me you could also ask why would anybody want to read anyone else's poetry? They are the same, in a way; kind of cryptic non-linear stories that take images and create something to be interpreted. After trimming out some of the uninteresting and poorly transcribed dreams it is, in its final form, almost 700 pages and is published in 2 volumes. They are for sale individually.

A dream from 33 Years of Dreams:

I was with a pet, female, smiling Buffalo and a group of friends hanging out in the country. And with an alien friend who materialized to be with us. There was a river scene, after going through a gate. Rednecks were hassling us, then we saw three of our women being physically abused down the road a ways, by three men. We headed down in force (with our alien and Buffalo) to deal with it.

Where to Buy the Books

To buy the books in print go to my Author Page: http://books2read.com/rogergoldenbrown

Versions of these books in eBook format can all be found at Smashwords, as well as free sample downloads: https://www.smashwords.com/profile/view/Rogue17

Check out my Smashwords author interview here: https://www.smashwords.com/profile/view/Rogue17154

Appreciation

A warm thank you and appreciation for all the friends that were there for me along the way. Especially Karin, Russ, Fred, Keith, my brother, mother, and father, George School, Santa Cruz, and all the water I have swum in.

Please contact me should you want to comment or ask about anything. Also I would appreciate any feedback if any typos are discovered.

wordsmith@goldengalaxies.net

Thanks for reading.